Pines and mist, Point Lobos

THE PRIMAL ALLIANCE: EARTH AND OCEAN

On further acquaintance, the place I live in seems to extend its boundaries and add to its store of lives. I struggle to understand. The more I add to my list of things as time goes on, the less my crude interpretations fit the circumstances. I started here with a tract of land. I built a house. I have a family. I am not yet sure of my location.

I had been walking with my son, then five years old, and after a while he mentioned a house we had only just seen, in the way that children do before they have been trapped by the problems of time. "Remember?" he asked, as though it had not been fifteen minutes but months or years ago. "Remember how it was?" And I realized just how caught up with present anxieties I was—poor preparation for a season that called me out so beautifully. How can a man like myself, soaked with news, his senses muffled, shielded by the mechanics of his civilization and worn into despair by its brutalities, how can he know the real earth when he meets it? How can he be fit company for it?

Suddenly, we have left behind the conquerable wilderness which forced us into a fighting and sometimes loving relationship with nature. Subsistence farming, the self-sufficient locality, the man with his own mountain or his own shore, are not to be depended on for guidance. So we are world-widers, and haphazard ones at that. Who was responsible for letting loose the insecticides? Well, I for one. When the spray cans came out on the open market with their solution to everything from the potato bug to the clothes moth, did I not have my shelves full of them? Who drives at high speed over crowded highways at the risk of his neck? Well, I cannot be self-denying about that.

Do I not accept the power, and the energy, the mobility of the civilization on which I depend? I complain, yes, but I am a dependent, and I might even draw some excitement out of the idea of a new universality through knowledge and communication. But I am none too sure of the grounds on which I stand. How wise do I have to be to own pesticides, detergents, barbiturates, cars and guns, and how wise are they who provide me with them? The truth is that the possible consequences of my own ignorance, or idiocy, carried out on a global scale, stretched from the spray can to the hydrogen bomb, are almost too much for me to contemplate.

But I know that the field of life is still out there, not only ready to endure the analyzer, but also in wait for the hunter, or lover in us, as if no one had ever come before. It is a vast area of unguessed beauty and sensitivity. How can we be sure we will not find ourselves there again?

I began to hear its various singing,

the profound forms moving through water and air,

the sounds of a major unity.

lines from the Atlantic shore by JOHN HAY

photographs of the Big Sur coast by RICHARD KAUFFMAN

foreword by DAVID R. BROWER

edited by KENNETH BROWER

The Primal Alliance:

Earth and Ocean

FRIENDS OF THE EARTH ☉ SAN FRANCISCO, NEW YORK, LONDON, PARIS

A CONTINUUM BOOK / THE SEABURY PRESS NEW YORK

CONTENTS

SIXTY COLOR PLATES

We are grateful for permission to reprint excerpts from earlier
writings by John Hay:
Nature's Year and *The Great Beach, In Defense of Nature,* by John Hay.

This Friends of the Earth/Seabury Press printing contains corrections
of minor errors but no substantive changes in text, photographs, or
other illustrations. For current information about what is happening
in the earth's wild places, write Friends of the Earth, San Francisco.

Pine bough, Point Lobos

Foreword

THE PRIMAL ALLIANCE, EARTH AND OCEAN, and the series of which it is part, "The Earth's Wild Places," are intended to be part of an unchauvinistic American response to an American challenge in this way: The people of the United States use about half of the earth's natural resources and many of them seek a larger share still. The inequity is yet more disparate, because a small fraction of those people (I am afraid my family and I are among them) use most of that half. The aggregate result is that the American Dream has almost been polluted out of a place to be dreamt in, and a better one, that can leave all people with a livable world, needs to be dreamed. Those who make problems should propose solutions. In offering some here, I realize that it is bad to be didactic and worse to be presumptuous, and if you are about to be both, as I am, you had better admit it, explain, and hope for clemency.

Faced with the Now-Or-Never Seventies, what course would you take if yours were one of the greatest burdens of all, that of the President of the United States? Whatever his achievements and failings, he must keep more than half the populace behind what he does lest he lose the opportunity to lead at all. If you were he, how would you address your directors, the public? How would you ameliorate the feeling of futility that is pervading America and the world? How would you encourage people to step onto the world's stage and play the role they must play, creatively, if we are to find the route to peace with the earth, with its life-support systems, with its peoples, and with ourselves?

This question is perplexing, and there is no oracle to go to. It is nevertheless a good question that each citizen hoping to be responsible can help answer. It is a question arising from man-made problems that men and women can solve. So what would you say, confronted with a threat to nature itself that is real, frightening, susceptible to treatment, and never before so severe?

If the job were mine, and happily this is unthinkable, I believe I should like the cameras and microphones set up on the Big Sur Coast somewhere near Garapata, late in a long summer afternoon. The camera would sweep the coast and zoom in on the podium. I think my speech would go something like this: "Let me begin with concern for the whole earth, but focus first on a small detail of the natural world." The color camera would move in on the detail of a broken abalone shell, and I would read these lines from Robinson Jeffers:

> . . . to equal a need is natural, animal, mineral;
> but to fling rainbows over the rain and beauty above the moon,
> and secret rainbows on the domes of deep-sea shells,
> not even the weeds to multiply without blossom
> nor the birds without music . . .
> Look how beautiful are all the things that He does.
> His signature is the beauty of things.

Then I could continue: There will be no one to read His signature. There will be no America, nor will any other nation or people endure, on a dead planet. All nations, our own in the lead in an unhappy race, have been treating this planet as if we had a spare, and as if nature were our enemy. Each of us, as a human being, arrived on this earth to find it a miracle and a treasure, to find it a source of all the beauty that we know, and we are now discovering ourselves in the midst of almost having squandered this treasure, losing in the bargain any chance ever to know it again.

We have glorified man's acquisitiveness, his aggressiveness, his search for convenience and comfort and security; we have not thought hard enough about his ability to love and to revere life. Because criticism of what we thought was good enough has made us uneasy, we have stifled the creativity and the new thinking the world needs without quite realizing that this was what we were doing. We thought that the formulas that have brought us to our present success—and to our present brink—were all that we needed to sustain us and to rescue us.

There is need for change. There is still barely time for change. With fair application of the youth and imagination that should lie within each of us until we die, we can make this change and be delighted and pleased by it.

We need and, if we strive for it, we can have a New Renaissance. Let it be informed by the insight of the late

Adlai Stevenson in his last speech, one given in Geneva in July 1965. Let this be a universal pledge of allegiance to this planet and to its peoples: "We travel together, passengers on a little space ship, dependent upon its vulnerable reserves of air and soil, committed for our safety to its security and peace, preserved from annihilation only by the care, the work and, I will say, the love we give our fragile craft. We cannot maintain it half fortunate, half miserable, half confident, half despairing, half free in a liberation of resources undreamed of until this day, half slave to the ancient enemies of man. No craft, no crew can travel safely with such vast contradictions. On their resolution depends the survival of us all."

The peril to this planet, this fragile craft we share, and to ourselves is a tremendous peril, one that we are only now beginning to perceive fully. Let me try to put the peril in an understandable scale, a scale something like that which was made available to the world through the Apollo missions. To the intrepid voyagers to the moon, the earth was an oasis in the vast desert of space. The French underwater explorer, Jacques Yves Cousteau, who has plumbed another kind of space, has said that if we were to reduce the earth to the size of an egg, the water of all the oceans would be a single drop of water on that egg's shell. The drop would be about a fifth of an inch in diameter, since the oceans average 1/2800th the depth of the earth itself. The atmosphere, if concentrated to the density of water, would be a sixth of the diameter of the drop of ocean. The crop-producing soil that life counts on would be a sixth of the diameter of the drop of air and hardly noticeable to the naked eye. The drop, droplet, and speck are what make our planet unique, and our very numbers and appetites threaten it as it has never begun to be threatened before.

Let me explain why I say that. If you let the earth's 25,000-mile circumference represent the earth's age of 4½ billion years, each mile represents 180,000 years. Let's fly the great-circle route headed southeast from Dulles Airport and look at the time-perspective as we fly, to see clearly how long the earth got along without man, and how suddenly, in his most recent period, man and technology are exploding.

We take off from Dulles on our 25,000-mile journey the day the earth begins. We travel 6,000 miles (representing a billion years) before there is any life on the planet. Halfway around, just west of Australia, life has become complex, diverse, stable, and probably beautiful to whoever was looking at it two billion years ago. Two hundred miles west of San Francisco, after 22,000 miles,

we find that stone crabs and cockroaches have been added to the life inventory—and they are still with us. As we touch Kansas air, the age of reptiles begins and as we near Indianapolis it is over, but redwoods and pelicans have arrived. Just short of Cincinnati, whales and porpoises gather on shores and go back to sea. Our craft lets down and we are 6 miles from the runway before man appears. From touch-down almost to the end of the two-mile strip, man gets along with tools no more potent than a shaped stone, without enough energy behind it to interfere appreciably with the rest of the environment. With 400 feet of runway left, man discovers a simple agricultural technique and applies it in Southeast Asia. The Great Pyramid is being built and California's oldest bristlecone pine sprouts 150 feet from the runway's end, Christianity begins 58 feet from the end.

The purpose of this whole analogy comes next: Not *until the last 6 feet of our 25,000-mile journey did the Industrial Revolution begin.* In 72 mere inches man devised and used the tools that withdraw the biological capital of the earth and spend it. Before that he had lived on the earth's organic income without destroying or otherwise putting capital out of action.

Just a few more details: A foot from the end of our trip man began using DDT and chemical allies in his war against competing forms of life—a war the world's life-support systems had managed very well without theretofore. In the last 15 inches the earth's population doubled and California's quadrupled. In the last 4 inches, the world used half of all the oil ever used. In the last inch enough people were born to populate a United States. Our own life span gives us just two feet to stand on.

We are at this moment at the end of the runway and no one has proposed that we slow down. In fact, we have been asking for more speed. What kind of trip are we arrogant enough to think we can undertake next? Some of us are now planning to make demands that in the next ten years (a mere king-sized-cigarette length past the runway's end) will equal all the demands we have made thus far: the oil and power industries plan to double their output in less than a decade, to spend as much in the next 10 years, and produce as much, as they have in all the world's history.

Too many people, in overdeveloped, underdeveloped, and normal nations, are counting on some kind of technological magic that will let us stretch a finite earth and keep doubling the demands we place upon it for things. We will discover no such magic, no perpetual-motion machine, much less one that keeps accelerating. We must instead take a hard new look, in the coming years, into

Rocks and seaweed, Point Lobos

how we may live within the earth's income, and not continue to live beyond its means, and thus beyond our own.

The earth's income consists of the annual dividends available from the biological wealth the sun lets the planet and life create. We have been spending capital furiously. We can no longer hope to be forgiven for knowing not what we do. We can now see what we are doing to the earth and can ask with Thoreau, "What is the use of a house if you haven't got a tolerable planet to put it on?" The time has gone for undertaking vast projects without first asking, What does it cost the earth?

This question must inform us as we study our energy needs, our transportation, our development of food, our restoration of cities, farmlands, and forests, our renaissance of small towns and little crafts, our preservation of parks, wildlife, and wilderness, our approach to the population crisis, pollution, growth, the yearning for more and more things. It must guide our use of international relations and natural laws that can lead to peace, including peace within our own land. We do not need departments of environment nearly so much as we need governments of, by, and for people awakened to the need to preserve, restore, and respect the life-support system. That system enabled the world to work before man came, and it can let him remain here.

The ability to perceive is important too. Thoreau had it when he looked anew at a resource available to all: "The world has visibly been recreated in the night. Mornings of creation, I call them . . . I look back for the era of this creation not into the night, but to a dawn for which no man ever rose early enough. A morning which carries us back where crystallizations are fresh and unmelted. It is the poet's hour. Mornings when men are new-born, men who have the seeds of life in them."

Henry Beston developed the same theme. "Creation is still going on," he said. "Creation is here and now." He saw man as part of the endless and incredible experiment, to whom "poetry is as necessary to comprehension as science. It is as impossible to live without reverence as it is without joy."

John Hay and Richard Kauffman took this reverence and this joy to two different coasts and inquired into the forces of creation so beautifully manifested there. Where the shallows and salt winds are, where the land and the sea have most influence over each other, they watched the most important pageant, saw the sea breathing life into the land, the land nourishing the sea in return. But they saw that the primal alliance was flagging. The speed of its flagging should engage our attention.

"The wild sea, never the same," I wrote in a narrative for a film, "yet never to be changed by man." That was in 1956, before I knew how quickly things like Lake Erie could be killed, or that even the ocean would not be a large enough sink to handle the radio-nuclides, chlorinated hydrocarbons, poison metals and gases, and oil spills we have tested it with. By 1970, one would think, the world would have learned that there is no away any more in which to throw things, no great dispose-all on the ocean's floor or in its volume. Yet in the summer of that year, at the first Pacem in Maribus held on Malta, the alarm had apparently not been heard very clearly. The question asked there should have been whether man should continue to throw things into the ocean at an exponential rate and still hope to exploit the ocean for food and minerals at the same rate. But the question was not whether, or how fast. It was, Should the ocean be exploited by the many instead of by the few? There is no quick salvation by this route. International conferences might better ask what limits man must impose upon his tendencies to usurp the earth—what limits will take landscapes, diversity, wildness, other species, and man himself off the endangered list.

And on the wild coasts, where the primal alliance has worked so well so long, what should man's limits be there? There are answers to be found in the resonance between lines from the Atlantic shore and photographs of the Big Sur coast. In juxtaposing the work of Mr. Hay and Mr. Kauffman, poets from two different arts, Kenneth Brower has drawn upon his own still different art, finding mutual reinforcement in word and picture. It is a skill he has developed in the course of his work on nine volumes in this format, for the Sierra Club and for Friends of the Earth. His is a special knack in making wholes greater than the sums or their parts.

We are grateful for the artistry and inwit of these three men and believe their work helps prove this interrelated truth:

There is one ocean, with coves having many names;
a single sea of atmosphere, with no coves at all;
a thin miracle of soil, alive and giving life;
a last planet; and there is no spare.

DAVID R. BROWER

Berkeley, California
March 25, 1971

Introduction

HOW FAR do you have to travel to meet the miracle of life—all the way around the world at the speed of sound? Thoreau, in his journal, says no further than: "Here."

"Think of the consummate folly of attempting to go away from *here*! When the constant endeavor should be to get nearer and nearer *here*!

"How many things can you get away from? They see the comet from the northwest coast just as plainly as we do, and the same stars through its tail. Take the shortest way and stay at home."

Since Thoreau's time, human progress has done its best to shatter home and to break us out into the fragments and nerves of the cities, into the divisions of a nation, into the sky, into endlessly threatening realignments. Continuity seems to have lost its local assurance. But from our depths we must know what we have left behind. Along with our breaking out has come a compelling and even terrible need, one that comes from *nature* (let us call it by its real name), the need for the kind of cohesion and balance that brings the flowers into bloom and the societies of men into a comparable alliance; and this implies—for each of us—the need to name, and to recognize. If you have to travel, take your earth-home with you.

I step into a metally encased tube, which rises into the sky and drones toward California. The stewardess closes the blinds on the windows and a movie screen is lowered, three feet away from my face. The trans-continental route is closed, to the buffalo plains, the Great Salt Lake and the Rockies, the Navajo's blue bird of happiness, their early corn, the screech owl, and the golden eagle. Where has all the buffalo grass gone?

The wagons groan and creak, leaning from side to side. There are shouts, murmurings, coughs, day after day, through real heat from a real sun, across shadows drawing down at evening, and the hopeful lifting of the morning light. An axle is broken, the water is low, a child is sick.

They endure. They are hard and mean, kind and understanding. How does a man learn to accept what he endures?

I sneak a look through the blinds of the plane, after standing up and leaning across my neighbor, mumbling apologies, and there I see: reality at last! The range of the Sierra is loaded with snow, the breathtaking, staringly open, mountain haunches of the snow. Then, the movie over, we land at the San Francisco airport, right next to El Camino Real. In between the houses, massively clustered, or laid out in lines like the leavings of a paper chase, the long, wavy hills, indentured with ravines, are smooth with spring green, like felt.

It does seem, as you are translated from one coast to another—without much personal effort—that the noble advantage of a landscape is no longer at your right hand. You are obliged to try to find it, to make an effort in its direction, just as we now have to make an inordinate effort toward the living earth as a whole, or face the consequences. The fact that stretches of the California coast on one side of the continent, and of Cape Cod, Connecticut or Carolina on the other, have to be "saved," if that is still possible, is an indignity to them and has worse implications for us. How do we now measure our relationship to the earth? In what we see on television? That is too close, too hysterical, too perishable a view. You need a real arm to put around a real tree.

To see a coast is to live there, to live *with* it; and not to live with it is to be half dead. This is not a question of whether or not we can "escape" to nature any more. Wherever we are, none of us has escaped the laws of existence and the experience of what it means to transgress them, and we know this from the inside out and not the other way around. We have been dealing outside blows to this natal earth of ours. It is time to go back in and find what we are missing. There is no other place.

The masterful photographs printed in this book give

us the presence of nature, not in a lesser sense, as "unspoiled," but as eternal energy, variety, and order, subject to cosmic creativity. Nature is not to be conquered. Nor is it necessarily useful to think of it as set aside, like a refuge. Hiding out is not the specific function of this aisle of trees, this salt plant on the beach, or this volcanic wave. In the universe of life there is an indefinite number of holes and crevices, but in the sense that all its forms share in a common plan for realization under the sun, nothing is set aside. Whatever it is that requires renewal in plants and animals also calls for interchange and fluidity.

It is also true that man, the "successful" predator, is squeezing many parts of the earth so nearly dry that they are unrecognizable as resources, even to him who was once their product. We have made the American continent much smaller by our occupation. We have been successful, almost, in making one *here* very much like another, though nature shows a rage against any ultimate attempts at defeating her law of variety.

To impose such grim terms on our environment as we do, to foul its air and water, to restrict the sunlight and impoverish the soil, is to get grim results. Too much restriction is not only synonymous with violence, it may eventually cast its perpetrators out. No man can take the earth-ocean for granted any more. No more the romance of new worlds across the seas, new forms of environment to test ourselves against, no more the rich, clean swing of the tides to depend on, carrying a continually reliable sustenance with them. We went farther than we could have imagined, and we have no clear idea as to how to return to the great wilderness that widened our imaginations, even if it were possible. We have begun to discover the finite limits of the earth, in fact all our applied ability seems almost to have put it behind us, and we look back with something like terror at what we have done.

We have, for example, damaged a great deal of marine life, perhaps irretrievably, by the use of synthetic chemicals which will not break down through natural processes. The chemical industry values such nonbiodegradable chemicals for that very reason. Oil and oil products containing them persist in the environment for long periods of time, with lethal effects. The nature of the food chain in the sea is so complex that it is difficult to predict the resulting damage or threat to survival for each species, but that all are threatened is clear enough. It is also quite possible that a healthy ocean's importance to the ecology of that earth with which it interacts is incalculable, and may be essential to the survival of the human race. We know about the disappearance of haddock, or Atlantic salmon, or whales through overfishing. We know, or are beginning to know, the disastrous effect oil spills can have on marine organisms. We are also aware of the decline of certain species of birds, such as the brown pelican, the peregrine, and the bald eagle, because of our use of pesticides. We do not know, on the other hand, all we need to know about the earth's capacity to sustain life. Where does it stop being willing? Nature's power of regeneration has always been heartening and miraculous. We have depended on it, even worshipped it. But now we are capable of polluting and otherwise damaging the environment to the extent that the earth-ocean might not be able to recover if it goes on being subjected to such treatment. Nature, it appears, can heal itself only if the rate at which pollutants are added is not greater than the environment's rate of recovery. After that limit is exceeded, deterioration sets in fast, and may be irreversible. In the long run this deterioration may have advanced too far for us to do anything about. Despite technology's attempts to keep ahead of itself, it is not we who wind the universal clock.

It seems to me that not until a social and cultural commitment is made to the idea that the survival of man and the survival of the natural world belong in a common equation, can we begin to recover from our present difficulties. What we have to "save" is our own relationship to nature. Everyone needs a re-education in his earth home; there is an emergency need in fact, both on the personal and community level, to recognize it any and every where.

The tidal worlds of land and sea are inseparable in their long rhythms from the communal tides of history. However arbitrary man may be as a species, he is inextricably involved with all forms of life—the term *non-human* should not be used so as to isolate one from another. To what else should we have recourse but the basic principle, in this realm of birth, decline and renewal, that not to ally is not to be? Again, it requires a commitment. There are those who say there is not enough time, but surely not to commit yourself very often hastens what you fear. It's a lazy man who will not accept his own origins.

The equation of man and earth ought to be more comprehensive, and understood in more senses than those used by science and industrial utility. We need to overcome a distance, without the need for speed. We spend much of our time inventing disassociated solutions for environmental problems that can only be solved on their own terms. We devote ourselves to finding deceptive substitutes for living, creative transactions between us and the planetary process. We talk ecology, but we have scarcely taken the first step toward applying it.

To know this great coastline, with its thousands of curving miles, with overhanging hills or dunes on wind-stunted shores, with the rich sea waters pounding, carrying multitudes of life forms, running by, to relate to the great properties of organisms and place, it is necessary to slow down, and take a walk. It is necessary to stop, look and listen, to accept the level on which you find yourself.

Here, watching the surf along the Big Sur or at Point Lobos, or *here* on the Atlantic shore in spring when silvery light stands glistening between the trees and everything in the world seems to be preparing for the word go—but gradually, with the most wonderful, grave assurance—here is an ultimate meeting place. The great sea lions lie like sacks over the rocks off Point Lobos and the bulls cough and roar, in their assemblies made of high order and necessity. High walls of fog swirl in from the sea during the late afternoon, and if you stand on a hilltop you may see them enwrapping scenes of distant cities, peaks and skies. The green slopes and beaches are accented with bright flowers, and the contours of the coast are such as to give a man places in which to wait and let things come to him, while the waves smack into coves and rocks beyond him. East or west, these constant, rhythmic statements can be found, the true pulse seen and felt in living things, born in the lasting currents of the earth, asking our recognition; and are we ready to give it? Our sanity requires that we do.

JOHN HAY

January 25, 1971
Brewster, Massachusetts

1. Persistence Economy

There is in these regions a turning and hesitating, a waiting evidenced in birds or men, slack tide and full tide, the sunlight showing and then fading again, color and light on the sea, changing, moving on the order of the weather. The tide, which shows here as a final impulse, the end manifestation of a great tidal wave in the open ocean, a blister on the earth's surface pulled by the moon, is tangible. It tells men when to go out and when to come in, although the men I have watched along the shore, pulling their boats out at just the right time before ice moves in with the tide, or before a flood tide, and as they set out and come back with rhythmic assurance, do not need to be told.

There is a fitness in natural experience, an intimacy, that may not be superseded. How many, in this world of devices, now live through a lifetime of tides, nights of clean wind and clear stars above the roofline, know genuine exposure to cold rain, cold water and stiff fingers, know how to be steady there?

We are not nearly on the close speaking terms with nature that we used to be. Common naming, common names, are less familiar. Timberdoodles, shitepokes, ragged robins, skunk coots, wall-eyed herring and quawks are disappearing into books. How can the three-quarters of our population that lives in cities replace such terms, and all the humorous, rough, gentle, accurate acquaintance they imply? Common naming means a common recognition that numbering will never find. The object needs a person, to be personified.

The natural environment lacks the security of our once familiar speech, and we have also become less amazed, perhaps in the process of this loss. The earth no longer comes before us in a new aspect with every hidden flower and every earth-regenerating clap of thunder. We have left a great deal of awe behind us. The fact that we can alter and remake the environment almost at will has deprived us of much of our original surprise in its manifestations, even though it kicks back at us from time to time. To be a "free agent," in idea if not in fact, is to be tempted into monumental carelessness.

It is certain that the closeness of men and the natural earth as we once knew it, in the sense of local need and local routine, is largely going. There are still fishermen who are with their fish, in cold, raw weather, and people to whom their daily bread is a blessing because they have baked it themselves, but they have become scarce. Sowing the seed, watching its growth, struggling, in and around the year, with the exactions of the year, has relatively few practitioners. There may be no use going into mourning for hardscrabble farm, but the anonymous company which replaced it has no better hands with which to take up a hoe, or eyes for the wind. The farmers and the fishermen were often highly skilled professionals. They learned a reality, and they learned it in terms of living with place . . . something that is not taught by substitutes, on short acquaintance.

Have we become so megalopolitan as to lose our innate responses to whatever distinctive part of the earth we call home? Fiddler crabs have been transported from one coast to another, with entirely different tides, or put in receptacles of still, nontidal water, and their behavior has continued to be timed exactly to the tidal rhythms of their home flats. Then, gradually, though they were as insulated from the outside as a scientist knew how to make them, they sensed the atmospheric changes around them and adjusted their reactions to the lunar periods with which such changes are rhythmically allied. Insulation, self-installed, seems to work better with us in keeping us detached from the inner rhythms and senses of this planet. We seem to have lost the kind of inner timing which makes the plant react to the changes in the season, which sends the migrant herring or salmon to find its home stream, or the tern to leave a northern coast and fly down the shores of an entire continent. We still have the tides in us of our natal blood, but I sometimes wonder whether our conscious correspondence with them has not been left behind.

Cypress, Point Lobos

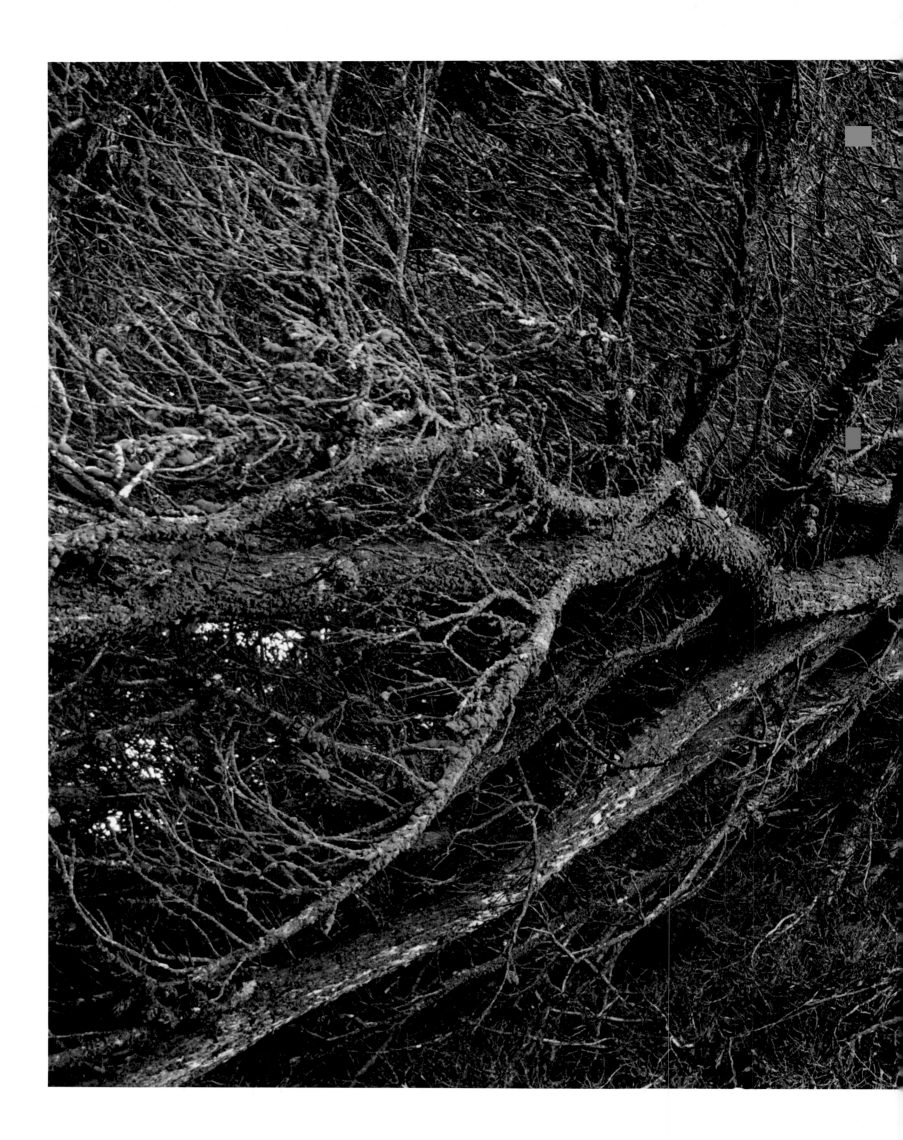

One of my regular stops along the coast, where my family takes its vacations, is on the shores of a cove in Maine. Almost every day when we are there I can see one old man walk down to the town landing to dig clams. He has been doing it all his life. Slowly, with shoulders bent, he walks down the road from his house. When he gets to the landing he picks up two hods, wooden, slatted, clam baskets, and then moves down to the rim of wet, gray tidal flats, made of muddy clay and stones and a residue of shells and detritus and starts to dig. Or else he gets into his old skiff, starts the outboard, and heads off to a farther stretch of shore around the borders of the wide cove, an inland entrance to tidal waters rising in and ebbing back through inlets and islands out of the open sea.

Aside from a few lobster pots which he tends, and a few dollars which he may pick up for pulp wood from his own already skinned land, clamming is his almost constant occupation, even during the winter months. This same area once had a soft-shell clam industry which occupied many men and was valued at $150,000 a year. Now there are only a relatively few men who moor their boats just offshore and make as much of the tidal grounds beyond them as they can, fitting their efforts to the vagaries of the market price from year to year and the fluctuating supply. For the amount they receive they need very strong backs, or some extra means of earning a living. Digging clams is part of a persistence as much as subsistence, economy.

Just a few miles down the shore, where towns or boating areas are located, shellfish may be put off limits at any time, banned because of pollution. Because of many years of over-digging and bad digging practices, the clams are in fairly short supply to begin with, though they have a remarkable power to recuperate. But lamentations are not althogether in order for a trade through which men can still have a hand in what they gather. The clammers may not be as deprived as some of the rest of us who are ignorant of the kind of communality that goes with food gathering. When the men, young and old, come in with their dories to meet the wholesaler's truck, any onlooker will soon see and hear that there is amity and rich experience in the collection and distribution of the soft-shell clam. There is a touch of freedom to clamming, a leftover from an earlier day whose local worlds were large and self-sufficient, not dependent on a vast, impersonal market, less affected by needs not visibly connected with their own. For all that can be said about the narrowness and meanness of rural life, men talked together.

That freedom was not only what the Glorious Fourth meant to a small town but it was also that of a casual fisherman, who had no special hours but worked when he wanted to, and when weather, tides and food supply permitted him. He was a man who would have a hard time adjusting to regular hours and a steady job. He had a special working arrangement with the world of nature. He cherished some secrets with relation to it, and had a corresponding inner weather. Such a man has been deserted by the world. Some of his descendants, inheriting the casual, may have lost the freedom, and their idleness lacks support. It is like those teen-age country boys who spend half their time racing up and down the road in old cars, which they fix up with spare parts and then discard, leaving their wreckage strewn in the fields. An angry deprivation shows in them, often directed at a world that races off in the distance on its own indefinite ways, beyond their means to connect with it. They act obliquely toward it by taking out the wreck, gunning the motor, roaring down the road and back again.

Meanwhile, the old clammer, still threaded to a poor but perhaps more stable past whose values seemed to grow by slow accretion, walks slowly down the shore. In a world of space-time, his is a one-place, life-span continuum. While satellites take pictures of the earth from twenty-five thousand miles up as it revolves through space, covered by swirling clouds, the old man sits down on a rock to rest. While laboratory minds, aided by computers, project their causal methodology into the future, he may be dreaming of the past. While science moves toward harnessing the methods of the sun through nuclear fusion and attaining unlimited energy for mankind, he stands, legs apart, head and shoulders down, intently and thoroughly digging away with his clam fork, working over the ground section by section.

Eroded rock, Point Lobos

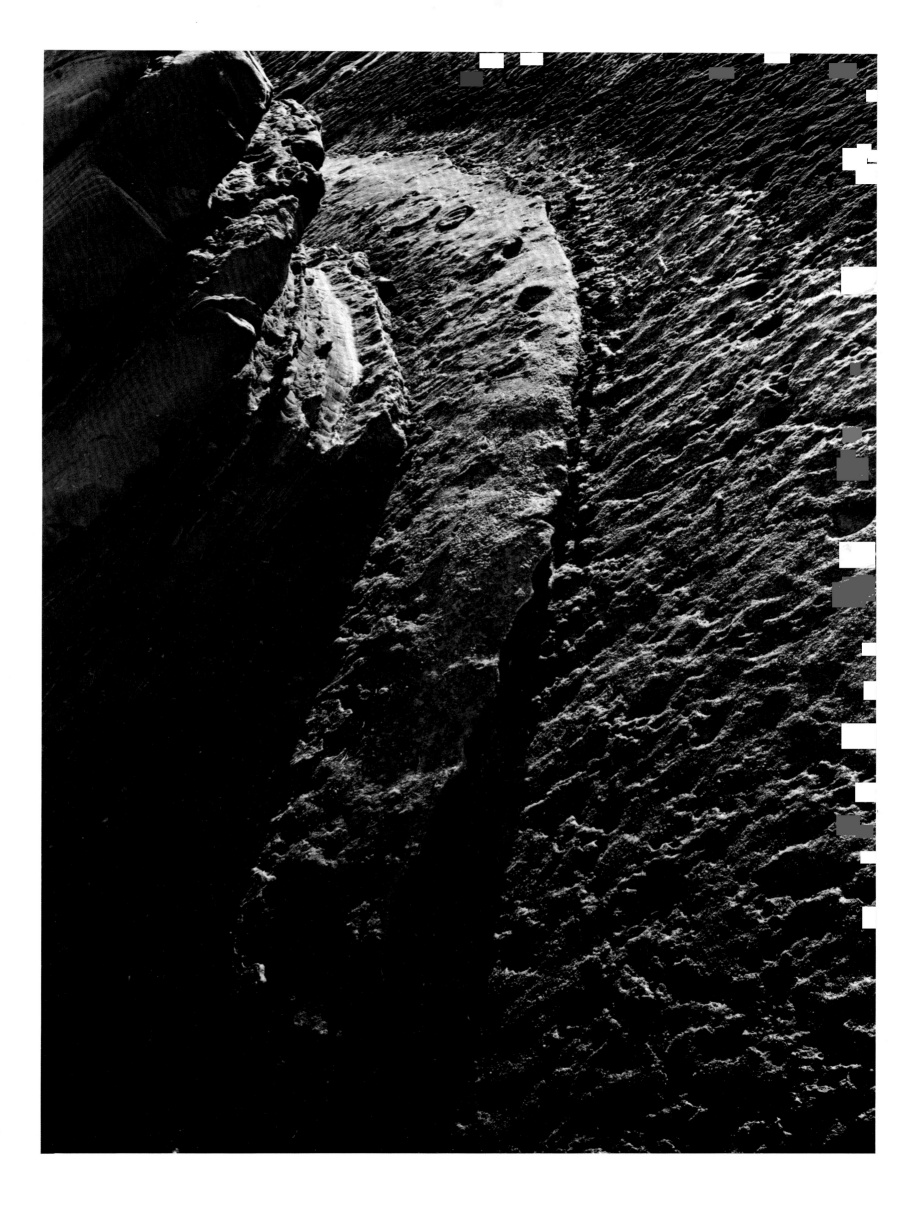

2. The Great Bypassers

Extra-human, extra-natural terms divide us from compassion. We have a death-dealing capacity that is without parallel; and, having to a large extent disorganized the gradual, assimilated experience which bound man to place, we have thrown events not only into the hands of unpredictable change but into the unknown capacity of mankind to keep control without appalling tyranny. We are governed by our obsession with means. We have been treating the earth with a recklessness which is no tribute to human genius.

I wonder, when men talk about their lonely fate on the friendless shores of the universe, faced by a savage nature which they can deal with only by taming, whether they are not really extolling their helpless pride? When a whole civilization is bent on eliminating "the undesirable effects of the external environment," including bites, storms, animals which compete with man for food and space, "trash fish," "weeds," vines that trip you up, and old age, it is applying wholesale methods and should expect wholesale results. What we eliminate is everything in the life of earth that saves us from choking to death on our own diet. We need the kind of dialogue with earth which does not always put us in the position of standing over the cash register telling everything else how much it is worth. We need to have the question asked of *us*.

Why this scarring business of playing God? Is this not our last chance to play at being man?

To make everything our own is to make too little of too much.

We have built up such fantastic material systems that they stand between mankind and all his original stars. We endanger the natural environment partly because we have made so many signs for ourselves, invented the means for so many accelerated directions, cut so many corners, that we have almost forgotten how to converse with it. And our greed for applications and appliances tends to make us forget that it was the search for truth and not its substitutes that made them possible in the first place. . . .

We find we not only have the means to destroy nature but our own world too. We find that our overwhelming position does not turn us into great communicators so much as bypassers. A kind of hardening and codifying of our methods and achievements seems to have detached us from the sources of life. Direct experience of the natural earth is becoming rare.

The road is behind me, the cottages, and in a few more miles a city, then a war. I live half in confusion. The way man's world goes is unpredictable. A society changes or comes into being as part of struggle and hope, and then all of a sudden we see what its terrible limitations are, what impossible heroism is required. We devour the earth with confidence and are surprised to find that we are limiting ourselves in the process. How will we survive our genius for invention coupled with our crazy willingness to destroy? Are we casting ourselves off from all biology?

There is a connection between man and the earth which is writ in water
but has more depth than we give it credit for. I watch the waves along
the shore for a force beyond exploitation, though I know we view
the sea they come from as a commodity, like everything else. The oil
drillers are after it. It is being used for wastes on a gigantic scale as we run
out of room—or perhaps the intelligent ability—to dispose of them on
land. The sea is being treated as a one remaining source of supply,
but not as it used to be, a hardwon if terrible friend. Since we can fly
over it in no time, that wide oceanic context is not as closely known
as it was to the men in Melville's *Moby Dick*, for example, as they pursued
their whales in open boats with the mother ship behind.

"It was a sight full of quick wonder and awe! The vast swells of the
omnipotent sea; the surging, hollow roar they made, as they rolled along
the eight gunwales, like gigantic bowls in a boundless bowling green;
the brief suspended agony of the boat, as it would tip for an instant
on the knife-like edge of the sharper waves, that almost seemed
threatening to cut it in two; the sudden profound dip into the watery
glens and hollows; the keen spurrings and goadings to gain the top of the
opposite hill; the headlong, sled-like slide down to its other side;—
all these, with the cries of the headsmen and harpooners, and the
shuddering gasps of the oarsmen, with the wondrous sight of the ivory
Pequod bearing down upon her boats with outstretched sails, like a
wild hen after her screaming brood."

Perhaps this smacks of cold physics, but to share (and that is what the natural environment needs of mankind—at the very least an effort toward mutual accommodations) may mean that we have to find new ways to tolerate the inescapable. After all, these global waters are where we came from. Out of these primal bounds and allowances the mystery of knowing emerged. Out of this life-sea came a being that could express the incredible idea of God in his hawk-headed heaven. Our limits and our possibilities have not escaped their universal origin, their ties in love. Life allows only so much, a certain number of seasons for any man. We are limited, but in major terms. Cosmic participation calls for scope. Reality circumscribes us, and at the same time not only awareness but the experience of living takes each of us on a great journey into space and into a profound, painful acquaintance with the relentless standards of growth and survival; and these are mere words compared with their potentiality. In us there is an infinite play in depth, of reckless encounters, brave effort, hopeless ineptitude, weakness that leads to murder and self-murder. But this is in the order of space, where we live on one earth and its many seas, room from which we will not soon escape.

As we diminish our environment, both physically and in terms of our attitude toward it, so we diminish our range of attention. Half the beauties of the world are no longer seen. What will we be when left to nothing but our own devices!

A civilization which isolates itself from its basic source of supply is weak in the limbs, and this is true not only in terms of what we call natural resources but of every living thing. What will the cities of man become when they are starved of a large part of the world's original company? The golden eagle and the polar bear are overtaken by helicopters and shot down. The lion and the antelope are dispossessed. There are only about a thousand grizzly bears left south of Alaska. The great whales have been hounded to the farthest seas. The fur seals are giving out. The wolf has been exiled. Lobsters, clams and fish are becoming scarcer. It is said that we will have to start farming the sea, which we are now filling with wastes and poisons on a major scale. We are faced with innumerable lost species and last resorts. At least mankind will have enough dead-end decisions to occupy it for a long time to come.

Perhaps we are more helpless than we know. Perhaps we are now on a convertible energy ride that will take us where it will. We may be part of a self-motivated evolution which is drifting us like plankton into the jaws of a whale.

Pine boughs and seaside daisies, Point Lobos

If the total amount of heat for the entire earth received during the course of a year from the sun were not in exact balance with the amount lost by radiation and reflection during the same period, the temperature of the seas and of the atmosphere would change drastically and ruinously. What a precise and nearly inconceivable containment that implies, where all acts the year around take part, and how dependent is the human race! At the same time how vulnerable we make ourselves, acting like furies to tip that balance over everywhere.

We have long cultivated the habit of thinking of the earth environment as having no meaning or application but what we give it. This cuts the earth down to a flat which has no bird tracks, or wormholes in it at all. The so called conquest of nature, which was made possible by nature's primal capacity to renew and provide, has almost put the human species on its own, a state of affairs which is getting us into more trouble every day. To draw on all the earth's resources without being able to give anything back is not an imbalance we could survive forever.

Oak tree and autumn color, Big Sur

Much has been said or written about the extinct passenger pigeon, and after all, clouds of them darkened the sky within living memory, and broke off branches of trees with their weight. Forbush wrote that "it was in some respects the finest pigeon the world has seen," and it was commensurate in its incredible numbers with the spread of forests across a matchless continent.

"They migrated *en masse*. That is, the birds of one great nesting rose into the air as one body, and the movements of these immense hosts formed the most wonderful and impressive spectacle in animated nature. There were stirring sights in this and other countries when great herds of grazing animals thundered over the plains, but the approach of the mighty armies of the air was appalling. Then vast multitudes, rising strata upon strata, covered the darkened sky and hid the sun, while the roar of their myriad wings might be likened to that of a hurricane; and thus they passed for hours and days together, while the people in the country over which the legions winged their way kept up a fusillade from every point of vantage. Where the lower flocks passed over high hilltops, people were stationed with oars, poles, shingles, and other weapons to knock down swarming birds, and the whole countryside was fed on pigeons until the people were surfeited."

There are few multitudes left, other than in the human species or the insects, which keep escaping our attempts to kill them off, to deserve the term "appalling." The tragedy is that many of the standards by which the majesty of the earth could be judged have been cut down.

The great danger in a revolutionary world that takes us with it in spreading mobility, forced communication and unprecedented speed, uncertain of the outcome, is that we will take our own risks and live out our own violence as we can. In other words, we may risk the habitable earth for the sake of mere impetus. Perhaps the awareness of disaster will prevent us from bringing on our own artificial ice age which could postpone spring for ten thousand years. Perhaps we can, by conscious, continual effort, keep turning the bow aside to save the ship. We will have to try, in this one world. We have now come to the point where we meet the living earth either in terms of fundamental conflict or fundamental cooperation. All our pillaging and presumption have brought us face to face with ultimate limits. We have pushed ourselves and the rest of life on earth to a point where one step more could mean survival or extinction.

Barn window, Carmel Valley

Our reduction of the multifarious parts of the landscape means a reduction in revelation for ourselves. Surely we are in need of all the variousness earth can show us. The texture of life grows with association, and not just with your own kind. Vision or blind touch are as incomparable in the rest of creation as they are in us. These lower lives over which we walk are not just part of some ancient dispensation which we can replace with our own. They are part of the wide and continuing energy of the present. They express, in their various sensitive ways, the interdependence of the earth and what it offers, what it does and says to us.

Sanderlings hurried forward at the line where beach and water met, almost shaking from side to side as they went. There was something about their twinkling forward and stopping to feed, their going on again, loosely and at the same time interconnected, that made me think of little fears running together for company. They acted almost as if worry were a part of their characteristics as a race. (I suddenly hear a voice saying: "Can sanderlings make gravity bombs?" That, as I understand it, is the latest projected advance in complete annihilation, and of course nothing on earth could produce one. We are special and even, if you like, unnatural in that—or almost with a Nature of our own. Yet what does such a weapon come down to but ultimate worry?)

One sanderling pecked quickly over the rockweed covering a big boulder offshore which was being rhythmically passed or hit by the waves. Just as a direct wave was about to break, the bird would casually flit into the air as if without looking, and then return. Farther along, a three-year-old herring gull was pecking away at a small flounder on a sandbar, pecking at it, lifting and dropping it again. A second flew in and landed near the first, which uttered a long call, while the newcomer stood rigidly by. Both called together, and the second, having obeyed the ceremony of threat and response to threat, flew off.

Subliminally, man's heroic and sacrificial terms may be struggling for an outlet, but we appear to have discarded our ancient symbols and taken to substitutes made of the base coin of the realm. Still there is something heroically unalterable about the spring. And when I hear those old languages emerge again, in a frog or a bird, when I see wild knowledge in an animal's eye, when I feel, at last, the earth begin to slide and breathe under my feet, I am not sure that we ourselves, even in our will and conscious ability, were not included in the embryonic vision of the year.

California poppies, Big Sur

3. Alliances

Many a wandering observer like myself, when the sunset at Pemmaquid turned the great sea-wet rocks along the shore into smoking barrows and fire pits, and the small things went into darkness, felt that his inner cognizance had far to go, that all he knew was an alliance without specification except that what he had survived so far was life, and that what he would not survive was life; but also, something in him, though he was alone like other men with little light, felt the hint of an incalculable creativeness at the massive depth of things, which might be a madness to touch upon.

We built a small concrete pool on our place, which is locally known as Dry Hill, and so brought the life of water a little closer to us. In the summertime the pool nurtures a migrant population of green frogs. I have put nothing in it except some sunfish that subsequently died, so that the occasional signs of new life it shows, like a water strider, or some nymph or larva of an insect that flew by and deposited its eggs, always strikes me as a dispensation from the sky. It is a proof of life's pressing, inescapable need to drive into every opening.

It took me a while just to learn the local compass directions, but now that I have my north, south, east, and west inside me, I am not sure, even walking through the trees, that I will not bump into my old ignorance. It takes time to find your way. A man new to the countryside might well be envious of some of the older inhabitants that know where they are without trying—a turtle, for example. A box turtle's slow motion over the year seems like a true measure of ancientness. While the birds, the fish, the men depart, this dry land reptile seems to feel responsible for holding back, for the weight of the earth itself. In the springtime I have seen a slow pair approaching each other in a mood of affinity, while the rest of the procreative world danced overhead, and I have seen a female laying her eggs in a sand bank, covering them over with a last shove of her hind legs, then moving away, a little more quickly than usual, it seemed to me, as if to return to the more agreeable task of waiting things out. When fall comes and their cold blood slows, they grow torpid and finally dig out of sight into the ground.

The wood had a climate of its own, cooler, darker than the hot, damp, wide open world of road and shore. There are climates within climates, as there are worlds within worlds. Under the bark of a tree the beetle inhabits a place that has special atmospheric conditions differing from the woods outside it; and so it is with the woodchuck in its hole, the ants in their hill. Any place, of whatever size, however endowed in our scheme of things with grandeur or insignificance, any home, may be greatly subtle in its variance.

I do not, or cannot, go very deep into what a cove or the trees above it may mean in their complexities, but the depth waits. From the centipede that makes its way through particles of soil to the tips of the highest branches the wood stretches from the roots, breathing, groaning, roaring if our ears could make its inner processes their own. Birch, oak, spruce, arborvitae, pine and hemlock, each in their way vulnerable because they have to stand and take it, unable to move like animals in search of better conditions of light, moisture and freedom from enemies, stretch next to each other, continually in exchange with their surroundings. Trees may not have "passion" attributed to them, but they endure as much competitive ardor, and disaster and tense exactitude as the rest of us.

There is no noise or compelling distraction in a field or stand of trees. Still, a forester suggested to me that if trees could make themselves heard, in their internal growth and adjustments, the roar would be deafening. The same thought has been applied to life on the ground, with its countless microorganisms, in a state of continual displacement and turmoil, growing and dying, consuming and being consumed. They too might roar. We have enough at hand and under our feet to make general tumult no surprise.

Dead cypress, Point Lobos

We very rarely assume that any such silent, faithful, available plant would be able to draw any more out of us than a tacit acceptance. On the other hand, trees breathe, a slow, quiet, tireless breath, exchanging gases with the outer air. They drink, through the elaborate network of roots that thread the soil. They apparently communicate impulses from cell to cell through the thin film of cambium just under the bark. They manifest the most sensitive and elaborate connections between the earth, the air and the sunlight. They are not only a life environment for native birds and squirrels and the thousands that thread the leaf mold through their roots, as well as a passive shelter for all travelers, but their connections with animate and inanimate things might just as well be called personal.

None of us seem to get the chance to see enough in order to rightfully enlarge our lives before their end. But we have a history in us which is of the earth, and nature gives us clues to its capacity, and signs now and then of the incomparable form and passion in which we take part. I remember, when I was in Nova Scotia, heading for Newfoundland, that I passed by a woods fire on the way to the airport. It was only a small fire and the local fire department had almost managed to put it out. The men were concentrating their hose on the ground at the base of a tall spruce, the last to go. The fire shot up in a deeply roaring, devouring orange-red wave. Then it topped the tree with a final rush and fury. A one last crackling curl into the air and it was gone completely, leaving a tall, smoking black stick with naked branches behind. In a country of frequent forest fires, this was not a memorable event, but for me it provided an added, elemental statement, flung out against the background of an ancient world.

Years ago, I first saw freshwater herring, or alewives, migrating up a brook in the springtime, and with some gradual learning on my part I began to realize that they held all earth connections in them, the sun and the moon, the waters of the sea, the land and its downflowing streams. One crowd of silver fish, one stream surface shaking with fins, began to lead me out. For a while I searched from day to day and year to year, and the phenomenon of migrant fish gained more depth as I went on, never far enough. When the fish arrive out of the sea in spring, it is still a first time for me, and I see in them a coming which is more than I understand. . . .

Intermoving, rushing occasionally, circling, curving and coiling, these heavy fish swam with the kind of flexibility and at the same time contained force characteristic of the moon-pulled tides, of a tornado, ice forming on the shore, the flower moving from its sheath. Also, I saw in their fixed destiny something which I had experienced, as part of a crowd, having to join the army, having to become a part of a war, having to go to school, to be organized, to be disciplined so as to endure, to migrate through calamity. There is a common tyranny in common life, and looking down on the alewives massing in a need to spawn that could not be turned back, I felt a precariousness that has no end.

The lines go out, infinite analogies are possible, the earth spins and recombines its forces, within the never completely defined cosmic order. Each success in human definition leads to another corner around which we have to define again, a spur both to vision and despair. Behind appearances, the city of man, the city of the ant, the flower and the weather, natural energy keeps burning.

Mesembryanthemum flower, Point Lobos

Bluefish Cove, Point Lobos

There is nothing in nature which is not some other manifestation of that incredible energy. It shines out in the wild flower as it does in our terrible and unexpected discoveries, but in nature's successes, its complete identities, there is also a precious momentum for any man.

There is no discrepancy between what makes me go through the same inescapable problems as my fathers, and the vast energies that are put into the readiness of the seed, or the sending of a mouse or bird through a short hard life for the sake of its race. These necessities come out of those down-under continents where indivisible existence was generated. If nature is inside me, with its grace and inevitable demands, I can hardly deny it without excluding myself from most of earth's intentions.

This putting forth of the gentle and implacable together in the realms of nature, the violet and the shark, of innocence to the ends of maturity, of rising up to send abroad, is part of world weather. And all the sacrifices made along the way are an immolation at one with all identity. Nature is life's creation, life's spending. No amount of intellectual despair, nihilism or sense of worthlessness in men can alter their basic dependence on regeneration, that which sends every beauty, each excellence, in each detail, into everlasting fire. We will not survive without the seeds of grass, and the mass of minute animals twitching in the waters of the sea. We belong to these multitudes; all that is lacking is our commitment and our praise.

The wide, warm-blowing new world is tender to the young, it is made out of darkness unlimited; it lunges precipitously like ravenous fish; it slips swiftly through the sky like a tern. At night whippoorwills by the dozen sound in the woods, with layer on layer of shouting song. Cold, wet hours follow, then nights with soundless soundings among the stars. Evenings are full of spirit fire like the feathers of a Blackburnian warbler, and ceremonious action, like the gulls that wait at dusk along the shore, strutting around each other, and flocking in circles overhead. Grand assemblies and fatalities, mood after mood, risk after risk, come into place. Like a thunderstorm in preparation, subsiding and coming on again, the season employs its prodigality, up to that controlled limit in the heat of early summer when the pollen stops blowing, the spring wind dies down, calm seas follow, growing life hunts and endures.

We share in this tremendous commitment, even in our own lavish use of it. While the blood of the sea runs as fresh as the juices in the plants and the pulse of living things beats high, the soul of the human world endures new trials. Every instant our being burns with infinite complexities. The context of the humanized earth is seething with change and disaster and renovation, for have we not been led by reckless springs for thousands of years to live in a wild way? It is a wonder the globe can hold us; in fact we may have gone too far already for it not to shrug us off. But by the same token we have the deepest need for all earth's measured balance, everything its calmest powers can provide.

To hail a herring gull, say hello to a clam, or take some vocal joy from the flight of a hawk, may seem eccentric. I have, on several occasions, spent time in the close company of an injured gull or crow, and once a brown thrasher. They kept their own counsel, to say the least, so much so, I think, that no patterns I had ever learned about from the writings of the behaviorists seemed to fit them. They had their cut of the cosmos, and I had mine. They had the refuge of their own jitters or the inability to communicate. But it is not that I have anything to say that would be useful to other animals, or even plants—after all I have a hard enough time in human society in that respect. It is only that I like to feel free to express our mutual company with or without returns.

The end product is endlessness. Every act and its revelation, a hole in the sand, the shaking of the grass, the scoter's easy riding, is composed of measure and the unmeasured alike. The hawk belongs to the earth's continuous making, and if I belong there too I see the hawk as one to another, I and you. It is not so much that everything has to be found out as that it still has to be met with. Along this same shore I have never had to assume a great deal. I have been given as much as I have found.

It is still possible, if you have time enough and inclination, simply to
watch and wait. All corners of the world that are not so restricted by
human pressures as to blind us to them have their revelations still in order.
The earth is full of junctions from the past and natural opportunities
in the present, whether fulfilled or not. These meeting places may
have their mastodons or dovekies, their egrets or their horseshoe crabs,
the fossils and their living relatives, the rocks of nearly impenetrable age
being washed by the latest waves. In these images, in this unmatched
context, nature may take a shape I have never seen before, so I
walk out again.

4. The Shore

Cold and sonorous still, the sea broke out,
And led me from my derelict dismay.
It stood me on the sand, throwing its white
Commandments at my ribs until I sang.

That music I remembered—past my stay
In wars and cardboard towns.

The tides rotate around the day, the year, the centuries, keeping their mathematical, graceful pace, to be reckoned accurately for whatever part of the coast we live in. I have heard it said that the tides, more than anything else, made men feel the imprisoning of the universe, meshed in its gears and no escape. But the wheels within this wheel are infinitely variable, infinitely discoverable. The overall weather roams and turns. Birds hesitate, fly out, wheel overhead, land and feed. The flock of buffleheads, white feathers glistening in gray light, suddenly whip up off the running shallow waters of the cove. Everything changes, gives, adapts at any given moment.

The tidal flats as a vantage point on the globe have more open space than most. They are full of storm tossings, regularity, the constant influences of world weather, beauties of reflection, changes in mood. Sometimes, as on autumn days, they summon you out of an evanescence joined with the whole sky. Their volatility is open to our own, even those waves of emotion which may not fly loose over a sandbar, or be useful to investigation, but are of nature and her sea sure enough. They invite me to an extension of myself, with no divisions of matter or spirit.

On some days the shore seems calm, compliant, restricted in dimension when the tide is in, while on others it springs with conflict and force. . . . At high or mid-tide the waters seem to run back and forth, seething with give-and-take, malleability and resistance. Wind strikes their surfaces, shifting and spreading them, cutting at them, turning and whipping. From the land's rim to where the waves slop on the horizon like water in a bucket, there is a wild stiffness and obstinacy, a northern energy at war with itself.

On other days I see all haze and illusion. The light over the flats on some September days distorts perspective so that a man coming toward you looks like an eight-foot giant. Way off in the hazy distance along the curving shore, cliffs and headlands show up as separated from each other across the water, isolated towers and islands swimming in the air. Waves coming up over the sandbar two miles away look like lowflying shapes. Groups of people at that distance, or the ever-present community of gulls standing into the wind, become either outsized or dematerialized. Reality becomes a mirage.

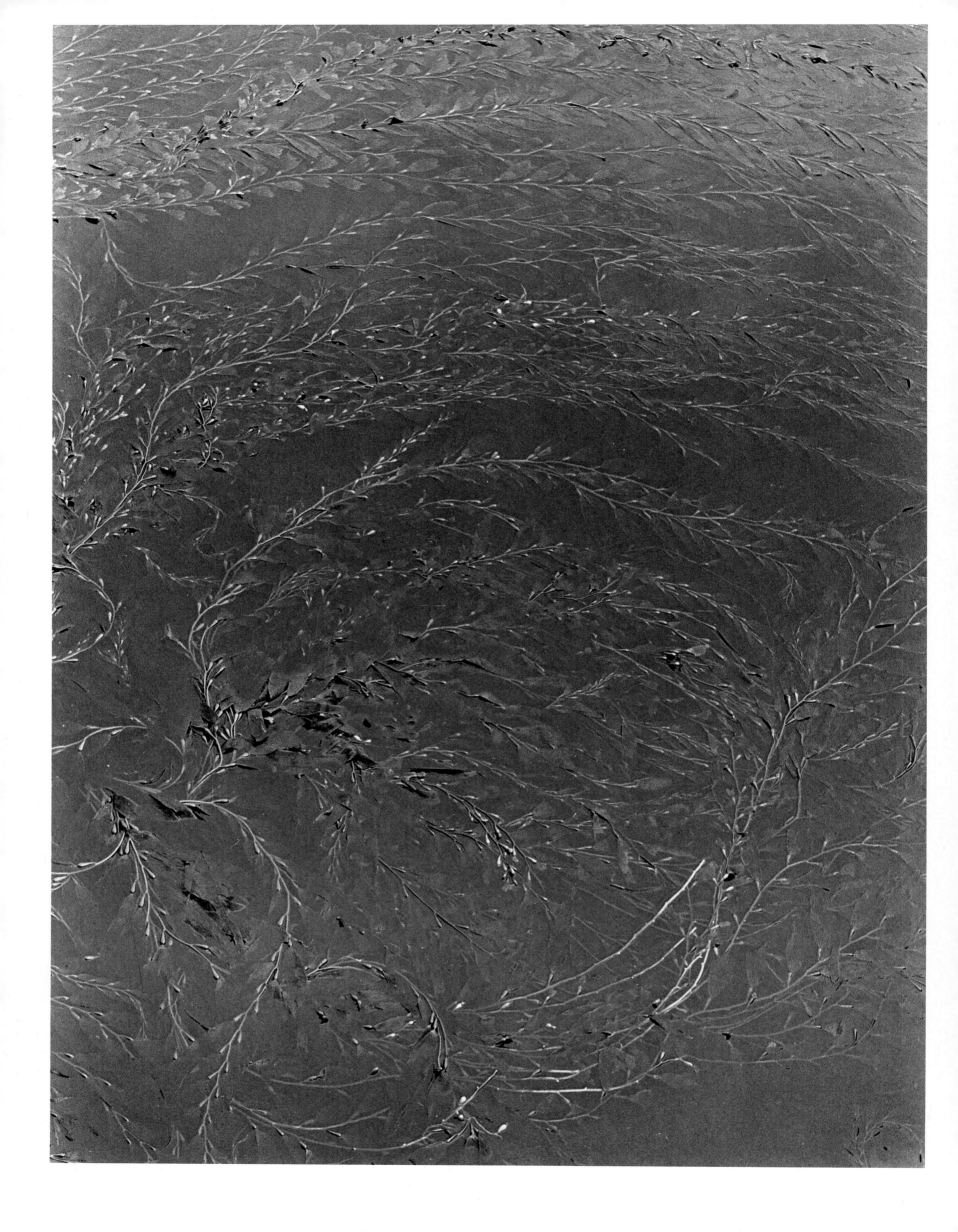

How hard it is, in such an age, to realize that the sea of life, the wilderness around us, is intrinsically, overwhelmingly calm! Perhaps that calmness shocks us, the way people are shocked by the will to live of a sandshark—its staying power is as disturbing as its voracity. The unvisited sea keeps its savage and capacious counsel. It makes the fish fry leap and skip in a silver rain across the surface, escaping their enemies. It makes the barnacles wave their feathery feet, and the snails crawl and the silver herring school. Its great shifting currents, dark depths and light surfaces, its varying bottoms, from shelves to ravines, its reconciliation and embodiment of temperatures, its running range, give quickness to some, slow deliberate motion to others.

Kelp, Point Lobos

Here is "function" in all variety, each life to its place, filling a niche, with the special form and manner by which it feeds and tries to survive. And every bird is a bird of the sun, adapted to this treeless, narrow shore that blazes with cutting light, the light of sand, or rock turned to sand, of water, roaring and moaning in the sea, rushing back through a tidal cut on the ebb, then trickling, evaporating, and swelling in again at the flood. Each animal works an open coast, across its burning days. The fliers with wings so sharp, energies of light, fit the high or low wants of the wind, the curves and sweeps of the open marsh, the glaring sands. And they hurry on stilts, or tiny short legs. They bob up and down. They run trippingly along—all to the rhythm of the watered, indefinite shore, looking for food that is rhythmic in myriad ways. Here is a great tribe of searchers.

Out there over the free waters, the bird dove again, and screamed.
A single dive, and success . . . and when I saw it my scalp tingled and I
connected with the continental beauty of it; the act was like a
hot iron plunged into the cold sea, and it joined the islands and water,
fish and sky together.

The water itself, that wonderful stable medium without which we could not exist, keeps running back and forth, flowing with its special life forms, its adapted secrets. It carries the shed skins of barnacles at times, so many in any small area as to indicate an abundance beyond belief. At certain times of the year it also carries minute newly hatched fish, quivering like tiny slivers of glass; their definite black eyes contrast with their bodies' transparency, so fragile as to have a power in fragility.

Underwater grasses, Point Lobos

There are so many unfinished depths suggested by the surface of things. A wet, white and gray pebble of quartz has the kind of grain that leads off to snow and rain and all the watery and windy associations of earth history. A feather, fitted, barbuled, light and strong, holding the air, refracting the rays of the sun and using them for its colors, has the horizon's curve and the graces of the sky. The bryozoans on the seaweed tell a deep and primitive tale about the salt water and its animation.

I may be able to assure myself, when walking through fields or woods, that I am in places where, as a land mammal, I can communicate with the inhabitants. I can also ally myself, anthropomorphically, with a thrush, a lightning-scorched tree, the prolific grasses, or almost anything else I meet, but the flats, in their primal flatness, their transparencies, their elusive organisms, seem in some respects like the surface of another planet. This is a foreign shore, except for whatever food gathering makes it familiar to me. I do not know a tenth of the inhabitants or how they live, eat and reproduce, or what their strange anatomies may mean. Some of them seem to have their hearts in their feet and their stomachs where their mouths ought to be. But it is very evident that what they are all obligated to is a standard of endurance so far as the world's shore environment is concerned. They live in regions of shallow water where there may be the most extreme variation in temperature over the year. Their greatest danger is desiccation when the flats are uncovered by the tide. They also have to survive storm waves, ice and heat, sudden shifts in the surface volumes of sand and mud which may bury them. For these burying little animals with twinkling legs, for these worms and crabs, life is drastic, pared down to essentials. They are closely allied with whatever bare principles in the universe call for the dignity of obedience.

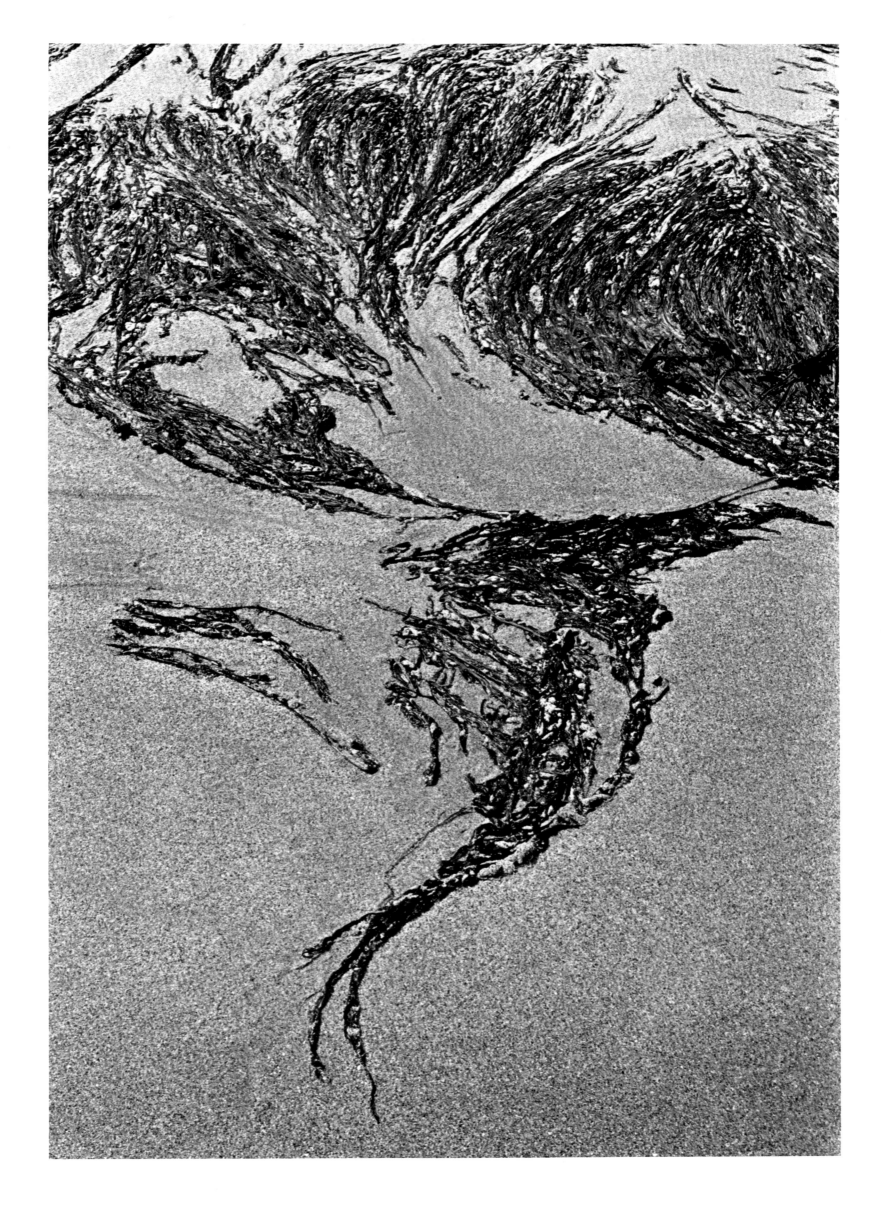

At first I noticed thousands of little mounds on the surface of the sand in a strip some six to fifteen feet wide along the upper part of the beach, following in general the outlines of the previous high tide. Where a log or shelving bank was in the way, these mounds, and the many holes accompanying them, about knitting-needle size, were concentrated on the seaward side. I noticed that shore birds had attempted to pluck the occupants from their holes and had reached down two to three inches. I scooped out the sand where a hole was, spread it around, and revealed a little animal not over a half inch long, with two large eyes covering the sides of its narrow head. The eyes were not only conspicuous, they were also startlingly white; and the sand-hopper's body, flattened on both sides, was a mother-of-pearl, somewhat translucent. This odd creature, one of a family in the order of amphipods, is called *Talorchestia megalopthalma*, a title that gives special credit to its eyes.

I put my pale-moon animal back in its hole, but to be held and thrust against its own volition apparently immobilized it, so I let it go free down the sands. After a second or two it made a few big and seemingly crazy hops—on sidelong springs like a toy—down a line of mounds and holes, popped into a hole and promptly disappeared.

I noticed that little spouts and bursts of sand were coming from many of these holes and with a little patience I could see some of the hoppers coming up as if to look around, as is customary with gophers and chipmunks, and then turning around and going back down again. What they were doing of course was a major job of digging, passing the sand up from one pair of legs to another and throwing it out the hole with a jerk. There was hardly time or inclination to pause and look around the far horizon. It was work that had to be done unceasingly, between tides and between seasons. Perhaps, if tomorrow brought consistently freezing temperatures, they might not appear again in any great numbers until spring; but their usual daily round meant frenzied feeding at low tide and after dark when no winged predators were around, followed by another return to the upper beach and another furiously energetic period of digging homes for themselves. Terrestrial animals, which might drown after a period of immersion, and yet bound on this strip of sand to the tides, they had a more legitimate claim to the beach than most of us.

There is a change in population at each tide. The resident animals—mussels, barnacles, softshell clams, crabs, worms that use the basic mud bottom for their burrows—use the food that comes to them in seawater, or move out to prey and scavenge, often at night.

But even the fixed, sessile animals like barnacles have larval forms that are distributed far and wide by the sea; in their case, all over the world. The incoming waters flush and drain, bringing in marine plankton, taking detritus from one part of this cove and inlet to another, stirring up the plant life, prompting animals to move about. It is a sheltered environment, but nowhere without motion, nowhere without response of one kind or another, in the levels of the water itself, on the surface of the scattered rocks and underneath them, through the surface layers of mud.

Among the many species of animals in this area there are all kinds of adaptations, to light, to excess oxygen or the relative lack of it, to wetting and drying out, and many methods of concealment or locomotion. The cove is an inshore marine environment of course, so it is not a self-contained unit like a pond, with its own population, and in part its own climate, irrespective of what lies outside it. The cove partakes of a larger mobility; it shares a distance, with the migrant smelts that come in early spring to lay their thick clusters of eggs over the small freshwater streams that flow into it, and with the tribe of herons and ducks, with an occasional seal, and the striped bass. For all its shallow waters, it contains multiple depths.

I have spent hours watching the tide flood and ebb, with an unfinished fascination at all the sand patterns in the making, remaking, or being left behind. This is water work, from the sea wave to the wavelet, out of depths into shallows, part of its vortexes and eddies, its inter-rushing and meeting . . . too much to catch. I am bound to be late, in this sea range where the water toward the north works the horizon and is worked on by the light, comes and receives all coming. The distance slips and ravages. Time and calculation move in a flood where we are left behind. With what ferocity we hang on to what we can get, to what little we can do! Still, the salty hour, the pulse, the immediate apprehension of these fleeting things, remain. There is a correspondence in us to those regular but indefinite motions of water and light spreading off over the curvature of the globe. Life allies us to a current that invites all distances.

Just so long as there is a wildness to find I can stay alive. It is not that I want it for an escape, since that is impossible in this world, but to share. The exchange of life is what is important. Unless we can see the "non-human" environment in terms of a whole that only acts, gives and receives fully when all its elements are in full play, then we will still be on the outside looking in. It may be that what we need more than anything else is to shake hands with the "insignificant."

Returning to the flats one day and trying to understand how the orbital motion of the water made ripples, I caught sight of a very small surf clam, lying on the surface. Five minutes later I saw it quickly flip over, slice into the sand edgewise, its anterior end first, and disappear, all in a matter of seconds. To have what I thought of as an inanimate, rudimentary object act like that startled me. It leaped into life. Clams, to those who have studied them with any care, are of course feeding, breathing, digesting, reproducing organisms. One biologist remarked that he knew too much about clams to be able to eat them. But to those of us who may think of them either as seashells or edible commodities, their status as living entities is apt to be low. That quick flip into the sands made me realize that I was in the presence of something else that not only deserved attention but added to the place where it existed. At least I was unable to say: "There's nothing here but a clam."

The unprotected, dry ground is eloquent enough of the assault made upon it, and the eroding cliffs with the plants that hold down the ground above them become part of the fierce sweep of time and oceanic weather. Here is a lesson in exaction. Perhaps those omnipresent Cape trees, the pitch pines, show the hard effects of a sea-edge environment more obviously than most. They cannot survive too close to salt water, but a little farther back the results of wind and salt spray is to kill their leaders on the windward side, dwarf them so that they grow flat on the ground like the Hudsonia, or to tie them in knots.

Everything has its method of survival. Each gradation of the ground, each hollow, slope, or level area, has a life to fit it or to visit it. The plants move forward seeking water. The birds fly through the thickets hunting seeds or insects. The exaction lies in a frame of reference. There is a quality of trial by the seashore, of odds, which taken care of by a mere plant, seem no less formidable. Their success in coping with the situation within its limits and precise needs is allied to all life's insistence on success.

It may be hard for a civilization built on waste to understand that, in spite of a vast mortality and a using up in nature, nothing is thrown away. The expenditure is not unilateral but for the sake of all things. Nothing is without its value, therefore nothing is waste. What appears to be merciless or cruel to us is merely a factor in munificence. This is like the sea, which may seem heartless to those who have to live with it directly. At the same time, men have always accepted it and even had a lifelong need for it. One slip into that cold, mountainous surf lunging against the rocks along the outer shores of Maine and Canada, and I might well be done for. I come back to stare and stare again at that vast roaming and resounding, full of a fire of associated lives, and it gives me back nothing but an anonymity; but I require it.

That one sea is both a builder and a destroyer. I look at the barnacles along the shore and wonder what can be said about these bleak, restricted lives, so lost in numbers. Along thousands of miles of rocky shores covered and uncovered by the tides there are often thousands of them covering one square yard. But it occurred to me one day as I saw barnacles in broad white bands and masses spread across the rocks that they were not only arrested, fixed creatures of their appropriate zones between the tides, but that they were an expression like the waves, spilled and breaking along the shore. They were living marks of the sea.

The seaways of soft feldspar green foamed and flew, and the clouds ran. Thin black strings of seaweed lodged in the sand were waggling back and forth in the wind. There was a swish of milky surf up the beach. Over the uncountable numbers of sand grains, each with its own size, shape, and color was a clean radiance, even a magic. Because in this realm of wide, majestic use, of continual advent, each offering was still of a proportion perfect for its moment in time. Each single action, the silhouette of the straw-colored grasses curving before the wind, or a gull shadow on a wave, a crystal grain sparkling in the light, was of such an excellence as to defy category or name. And they were magic and miracle in their shape and ways of use because they had life's inveterate sanction, and that above all else is not subject to lessening or degradation in this world of nature.

Like the lights that appear under the mist, or over the open barrens of the sea at night, like St. Elmo's fire on the *Pequod's* mast, there are electric tricks playing on the horizon, perhaps at all times, since there seems to be no end to light's action over the waters with the sky's depth behind it. As I walked up the beach there was a radiant white patch hanging up in the soft, scudding overcast, not in the sun's direction—reflected off the water perhaps—but having a wild aura of its own. It gave me a feeling of communication with something which had a right to awe. We may have passed the primitive stage, but the primitive respect for what was beyond human control and the magic used to propitiate it or bring it to play may still have their sources. The light and its manifestations is still too quick for the eye, or for the facts.

Science itself goes on proving that there is no infinite exactitude and that many things can be explained only in terms of probability. The fact that nothing is stopped by our constant search for a simple solution to life is what keeps science in business. The search into the nature of cells finds them full of inner whirlings, the motion of countless component parts, of a universal restlessness. They are structurally fantastic and each kind is manifestly different. Our voyage toward the invisible is unending. The molecule or the jellyfish, seen through one human lens or another, retain their share of the marvelous. And if we marvel, we are still capable of learning.

Gentle rising and falling of the tide over ribs of sand; swirling fogs; burning sun with spokes slanting down through clouds over the rim of the world, letting in calm soft lights, green and pink and pearly across sand and rivulets and pools, or cruelly glittering diamonds over the water. Light and water and wings flow in and flow past, the motion of ages, all actions being synchronized, as the hovering and diving of the tern is synchronized with the fish it catches, part of the indefinite combinations of things in a universe of motion. Over these waters and receptive sands life crawls or flies, dives, halts, stops, and starts, wildly, with quick hearts beating, or scarcely a heart at all, blind, or vibrant with sight, probing with accuracy and speed or merely moving at random.

They are all elements in a great exchange—this ardor and play of one instant in time, an instant that is equal in importance to all others. I stand here at the apex of one day. Here out of a thousand years is another advent, another chance for action, another use for sight, in the beautiful agreement of all contrary, separate, and divided things.

The tides change with their wonderful rhythmic grace, and life moves with them. As the tide began to ebb during the afternoon, with a simultaneous beating in and pulling back of low waves, a hundred gulls flew out from the salt marsh creek back of the beach, crying, moving back to waters now getting shallower, where they could more readily find food. It was a correspondingly rhythmic, well-timed, steady move. And so these backings and fillings, the going and returning, ripples in sand, a roaring sunset, a gray and showery dawn welcomed everywhere. Spring followed an ice age, the tropics arrived, a new ice age will be accepted in its time. The earth-tried enormous balance puts the whir of a fin and the shock of a hurricane together, and accepts all sinewy, kinetic, visionary response, and the inner darkness of sense as men know it— and the deliverance from sense.

Alongside my thoughts, my fitful advances, goes the enormous ease of all the waves. Then the sand sings a little under my feet, and I hear a muttering of gulls at intervals, and then the low honking of geese through the fog. I am aware of a global wheeling that never stops, taking the size of agony, the stature of trial with it. There is a corresponding spin in us which needs to be set going for survival's sake. I feel the earth's great vigor of deployment. The birds travel hard and out of sight. Fish circle and pulse under seawater. The earth, to include us, must have a passionate heart. I begin to hear its various singing, the profound forms moving through water and air, the sounds of a major unity.

For Ellie

A Photographer's View

SOME RANDOM and gloomy thoughts about the population explosion were brought on by a statistic in a recent letter I received: "With less than 3½ inches of California coastline per resident, the chance of acquiring any California coastal property at a reasonable price is rare." I let my mind wander nostalgically to the time in the late 'thirties when I discovered that magnificent coastal area comprising Big Sur, the Monterey Peninsula, and Carmel Valley. I remembered how one could then wander through the headlands at Point Lobos, drive down the Big Sur highway, or on the winding roads through the Carmel Valley, and hardly meet a soul. For me the world was young, and I was seeing its beauty for the first time. I was a color photographer then as I am today, but the bulky equipment and involved techniques limited my freedom of expression. I do not regret that I have saved no pictures from that period.

After many years spent with my camera in the Sierra Nevada, I returned to photographing the California coast. For the last seven years I have been deeply involved in this. Time spent with my camera at Point Lobos has been unhurried and delightful. I have been secure in the feeling that what I did not photograph today I could photograph tomorrow, or next week—or, for that matter, next year. This small State Reserve, some 1250 acres, is fully protected and not subject to man's destructive tendencies.

But with the Monterey Peninsula and the Carmel Valley things have been different. During this period I have watched with growing concern the sometimes gradual, but often sudden, disappearance of natural beauty. So with the photographing of these places I have felt the unpleasant pressure of having to move quickly to stay ahead of the bulldozers. The Big Sur, too, has recently shown the ugly scars of civilization, but fortunately much of the terrain here is too vertical to be subdivided. Yes, things are changing for the worse; but still much beauty remains, particularly in Big Sur and the upper reaches of Carmel Valley.

Like all people who closely observe the natural scene, I have my preferences. Although the choice is difficult, my favorite spot along these miles of splendid coast is tiny Point Lobos. It is intimate. With my own propensity for the detail, I find myself in tune with the grasses, flowers, tidepool minutiae, cypress and red algae, seaweeds, and the smaller inlets and coves. Some good luck and much foresight saved Point Lobos. On the other hand, tacky housing developments, hotels, motels, shopping centers, and ever lengthening and widening ribbons of concrete have spoiled much of the Monterey Peninsula and portions of the Carmel Valley. How does one combat the thoughtless acts made in the name of progress which slowly but inevitably turn our magnificent seacoast into a wasteland?

There is no easy answer. Nevertheless, a concerned person knows he must make his best effort. This may mean taking part in direct legal or political action, or at the very least, giving support to the activists. For a writer in the field of conservation it means the ability to impart the sense of beauty of the natural scene and then to instill in the reader the enthusiasm to do something about its preservation. I envy the good writer—and turn to the tool I use best to make my statement, the camera.

Many photographers feel today that they must focus on the ugly aspects of society. This Hogarthian method can be most effective. It is a valid approach, for example, when one is producing a photographic essay on a large city with its almost inevitable blight. To ignore this unfortunate side of our urban civilization would not be honest. But for me, photographing the natural scene involves something far different. The perfection of line and color in nature is so breathtaking that it points up its own moral. I see in the graceful curve of kelp on water, in the twisted yet strangely beautiful shape of a cypress limb, or in the symmetry and delicate blush of color of the ice plant a most powerful message for conservation in itself, a message that is completely effective without the juxtaposition of contrasting pictures of the more unpleasant aspects of our civilization. This truth is implicit in every one of nature's myriad forms; as I view their flawless line and color, they say over and over again, "Save me for the sake of humanity now, and for the sake of future generations; without natural beauty, the cause of mankind is lost."

PHOTOGRAPHY is filled with simple but rewarding pleasures for me, as, for example, when all the elements of a composition fall into place in an esthetic pattern on the ground glass of my camera; when I process a well-balanced set of separation negatives; or when I peel the third and final matrix film from the imbibition paper and see the Dye Transfer prints for the first time in full color. Uncounted repetitions of such acts over the years have not diminished my enjoyment one iota. Upon completion of a successful print, I am invariably filled with the same excitement as when I produced my first successful color print some thirty-five years ago.

My earliest memory is of my parents taking me as a child to a slide show, the first I ever saw. Amazingly, it was in natural color. I was thrilled beyond measure at seeing color in a photographic world that was then almost entirely black and white. For the child of today surrounded by television, Kodachrome, and four-color process printing, there would have been little noteworthy in what I experienced; but in the 1920's there was only a handful of technicians concerned with the intricacies of color photography. Later I was to find out that these slides were made on Lumiere Autochrome plates, the first really practical method of producing color transparencies.

Another early memory is of the delights of using a brand new 3A Kodak given to me in disgust by my father after he had taken several rolls of hopelessly blurred pictures on a trip to Yosemite. The 3A was a monster of a folding camera taking postcard-size negatives and featuring a sharp and fast (!) F7.7 anastigmat lens. I spent a few happy years with this instrument learning basic black and white techniques. It was not until the early 1930's, however, that I obtained a camera in which I could use the glass plates necessary for the color processes then in vogue, Autochrome and Agfacolor plates. Grainy in appearance, they were slow even by the standards of the time (needing one-half second exposure in bright sunlight).

I was not satisfied with transparencies however. I wanted to make color prints. They seemed to me, then as now, the proper goal of the color photographer. The Carbro process was fortunately brought to a high state of perfection in the early 1930's, and I soon adopted this superb method for making color prints. I have never regretted the many long hours spent studying color separation and Carbro printing techniques. Learning these intricate and exacting steps served as fine training for all my subsequent work in the field, teaching me, as they did, the discipline so necessary to serious color photography. Because of the costly time-consuming nature of the process, the popularity of Carbro unfortunately ebbed in the 1950's and the process was discontinued. Today, however, there is a high-quality process that has replaced it, the Eastman Dye Transfer process, a reasonably worthy successor.

I stress the making of prints because I firmly believe that a color photographer who is concerned with his work, who takes pride in the esthetics as well as the quality of his production, must make his own prints. The maker of transparencies is not a true color photographer since he abdicates his control of the final results to the rigid mechanics of a processing laboratory. The color photographer who produces his own color prints, like the black and white photographer who does his own work, can make an infinitely variable interpretation of the photographic subject matter. The printmaker can control the key (high or low), degree of contrast, warmth or coolness of tones, detail of highlight and shadow—all so that he can produce an image that speaks the way he intends.

In recent years I have gone a step beyond the color print and have involved myself in the production of four-color lithographic halftones for reproduction in books. In my photographs in the Exhibit Format book, *Gentle Wilderness: The Sierra Nevada*, I felt it would be a serious mistake if, after taking the trouble to produce Carbro prints which were my interpretation of the original scenes, I were to lose their subtleties in the lithographic platemaking process; so I set about learning how to make four-color process plates. Because of my training and background in photographic color printing, I found that by using suitable photographic masking techniques and the magenta screen process, I could make precise reproductions of my original prints and eliminate costly handwork.

In the present book I followed the same procedures. All plates reproduced here are from halftone separations produced in my darkroom, as close to the quality of the original Dye Transfer print as is possible by photomechanical means.

I would be less than honest, however, if I did not mention those skilled lithographers who helped me over the rough spots by their sound advice when I was first struggling with four-color process reproduction. They are: Warren Tuckmantel, Tom Peterson, Doane Gravem and Fred Ulfelder. Finally, I should like to mention with appreciation those craftsmen of the H. S. Crocker Company who, by their skills and dedication, took my half tones and from them printed this book.

RICHARD KAUFFMAN

Friends of the Earth in the United States, and sister organizations of the same name in other countries, are working for the preservation, restoration, and more rational use of the earth. We urge people to make more intensive use of the branches of government that society has set up for itself. Within the limits of support given us, we try to represent the public's interest in the environment before administrative and legislative bodies and in court. We add to, and need, the diversity of the conservation front in its vital effort to build greater respect for the earth and its living resources, including man.

We lobby for this idea. We work closely with our sister organizations abroad, and with new and old conservation organizations here and abroad that have saved so much for all of us to work for.

We publish—books, like this, and in smaller format—because of our belief in the power of the book and also to help support ourselves. Our environmental newspaper is "Not Man Apart."

If the public press is the fourth estate, perhaps we are the fifth. We speak out for you; we invite your support.

Friends of the Earth Foundation, also in San Francisco, supports the work of Friends of the Earth and organizations like it with projects in litigation and in scientific research, literature, and education.

Publisher's Note: The book is set in Centaur and Arrighi by Mackenzie & Harris Inc., San Francisco. It was lithographed and bound by Arnoldo Mondadori Editore, Verona, on coated paper made by Cartiera Celdit and Bamberger Kaliko Fabrik. The design is by David Brower. The Layout is by Kenneth Brower.

All colors, derelicts, and dancers fly
Above the currents of the grinding tide.
The sea bird's cry is sharp as water, while
The multitudes of night pass through the sky.

Billowing down like paper from the air,
The bird alights, to tremble by the sea.
A scale, it teeters on its needle legs,
And in its balance galaxies will share.

Under this ocean sky, while shadows trace
The moon, we join a kingdom's vanity.
With shining feet, all balance in our veins,
We dance away, as dancers take our place.